Simply Green Parties

Collins

An Imprint of HarperCollins*Publishers*

SimplyGreen
Parties

*Simple and
resourceful ideas
for throwing
the perfect
celebration, event,
or get–together*

BY

DANNY

SEO

HarperCollins books may be purchased for educational, business, or sales
promotional use. For information please write: Special Markets Department,
HarperCollins Publishers, 10 East 53rd Street, New York, NY 10022.

FIRST EDITION

Designed by Lorie Pagnozzi
Photographs by Jennifer Levy; Maura McEvoy on pages 18,19,20,24,32,33

Library of Congress Cataloging-in-Publication Data has been applied for.

ISBN10: 0-06-112271-8
ISBN13: 978-0-06-112271-2

06 07 08 09 10   ❖/QB   10 9 8 7 6 5 4 3 2 1

FOR ELAINE: *Every day is always a celebration with you.*

Acknowl

There are lots of people to thank for their dedication and hard
work that went into making this book.

Many thanks to Jennifer Levy for providing beautiful photographs, and
to Maura McEvoy for sharing equally gorgeous photos as well. A special
thanks to Kirsten Harris for her lovely illustrations.

To the supportive team at Collins: Joe Tessitore, Mary Ellen O'Neil,
Libby Jordan, George Bick, Shelby Meizlik, and Paul Olsewski. A special
thanks to my wonderful editor, Matthew Benjamin.

My adviser through the literary world, Mary Evans.

To the team that helps me grow: Emily Scofield, Tom Carr, Jessica Fee,
Matthew Lefferts, and Claudine Gumbel.

My friends and partners at LIME: There are too many of you to list,
but you know how proud I am to be working with all of you.

The Kimpton Hotel Group, the Rechargeable Battery Recycling
Corporation, and Method.

Last, but not least: Emily Baldwin, Jessica Brown, James Leland Day,
Nico De Swert, Rocco Dispirito, Norm England, Linda Gabor,
John Grandy, Theresa Hall, Sarah Heath, Rebecca Herman,
Kevin Hughes, Stephane Jaspar, Suzanne Koshnoodi, Jim Mannino,
Sean Mathey, Stella McCartney, Ralph Millard, David Moscow,
Rosalind Napoli, Kristi Nicolucci, Reshma Patel, Susie Perkowitz,
Pat Ragan, Jerald Richardson, Kevin Richardson, Maria Rodale,
Carol Sheehan, Amy Smart, Sandy Soria, Bruce Wagner, and
Kerry Washington.

edgments

Contents

CONTENTS

Foreword

When I first heard about Danny Seo, he was described to me as the Martha Stewart of the environment. Other than some obvious differences—he's male, he has dark hair, and, as far as I know, he's never had a run-in with the law—it's a very good description. Like Martha, Danny inspires us with design ideas that are smart, stylish, and affordable. But in his case, they are also all planet-friendly. He shows us that style and sustainability do not need to be mutually exclusive, and he is successfully turning the conventional wisdom that following a "green" lifestyle means wearing baggy clothes and ugly sandals on its outdated head. Danny is a remarkable person. He was born, appropriately, on Earth Day 1977. When he was just 12, he founded an organization called Earth 2000, which within a decade became the largest environmental group for teenagers in the world, with more than 20,000 members. His thinking evolved, encompassing entertaining, fashion, and home design. He has made living green not only doable, but also chic—more Calvin than crunchy.

As we confront the reality of our precious planet's dwindling resources, Danny shows us how we can help with a range of creative, elegant ideas for eco-entertaining along with a list of where to find everything you need. Not only should everyone strive to follow a greener, more sustainable lifestyle, but with a guidebook like *Simply Green Parties*, we learn how it can be easy, stylish, and even fun!

So what is eco-entertaining? It's using things that are either recycled or biodegradable, in place of items that are used once and then thrown away. Instead of relying on electric lights, or battery-powered ones, for an outdoor dinner, it might involve using rocks painted with glow-in-the-dark paint. It might mean cutting off the ends of Twizzlers and using them in place of plastic straws. Or replacing paper plates with ones made of recycled yogurt cartons or sustainable bamboo plates.

It is a host of ideas—many of which are in this book. But more important, it is a new way of thinking. It's a way of treating the planet as you would treat your guests—with care, compassion, and love.

Anna Scott Carter

Introduction

I guess I started off as a typical environmental activist, running a
national nonprofit organization and lobbying our elected officials to pass
pro-environment legislation. Outside of my activism, I also had a great deal
of interest in creating a stylish, comfortable home, cooking sumptuous
organic meals, and growing a lush backyard garden. Sometimes I felt as if
I were leading a double life. But as an environmentalist, I realized that
educating the public about living green meant asking people to make lifestyle
changes. Ideas about living in harmony with nature often meant giving up any
sense of style or fun. I set out to change that stereotype.

I've always believed you can combine style with concern for the
environment, and it doesn't need to be daunting or unattractive. *Simply Green*
is the embodiment of that goal—resourceful and innovative ideas that are
environmentally friendly, useful, and easy to do. Plus, and this is really key
here—they are *fun*. Saving the planet is serious business, but you don't have to
be miserable while doing it.

Simply Green Parties is filled with many entertaining ideas that you can use
all year round. These are projects I've been using myself (which means
they work!), whether I'm giving a friend a springtime baby shower or throwing
a winter dinner party. It is not about running to the store and buying
endless amounts of party decorations and knickknacks that just get thrown
out when the evening is over. A simple rock, for example, stamped with your
guests' names is not only useful, but it's unexpected and naturally beautiful.
Or take your energy-efficient solar path-lights from the driveway and hang
them high up in the trees so they cast a glow during an outdoor dinner party;
no special wiring is needed. These ideas are thought-provoking and simple,
and require basic tools most of us already have around the house. Not only is
reusing what you already have Simply Green, it is also simply inexpensive!

A Word on

Whenever a project calls for crafting materials, I have made a point only use readily available products. Nothing drives me crazier than reading a book that tells me to visit something like a cake decorating store—where I live, I'm lucky if I can find a decent bakery. So, everything I've used I found where I live. If I can make these projects here in the middle of Pennsylvania, it's likely you can, too, wherever you live.

I've also included a few recipes. While this book was never meant to be a cookbook, I couldn't resist sharing my favorites that complement the projects and make for even more fun. All of these recipes use readily available organic and delicious ingredients, and can be concocted very quickly.

I hope you'll see in these pages that being green isn't just resourceful, it's also plain old fun, too. Sure, throwing a party using recycled and environmentally friendly materials isn't the only thing we should do to save the world, but it's a good step. It's like that shampoo commercial: When friends see how you've thrown a fabulous fete using eco materials, they'll tell someone, and they'll tell someone, and eventually everyone will be thinking green at his or her next party. It's the everyday things we do (or choose not to do) that can have a major impact.

Warmly,
Danny Seo

Authenticity

A Special Note to the Reader

The Simply Green book series is printed
on recycled content paper and produced
without the addition of a dust jacket to save
resources. All of the photography is done
digitally, eliminating a significant amount
of wasteful film and processing, all without
sacrificing quality.

All of the actual props and materials used
to produce the book—from a reupholstered
chair to a gift-wrapped present—were created using recycled, thrift-shop sourced,
or truly organic fabrics and materials.
Nothing brand-new was ever purchased.
Even the colorful fabrics used as backdrops
in our beautiful still-life photos are 100%
organic cotton and hemp fabrics, often
taken from my own house.

Party 1

DINNER UNDER
THE STARS

Growing up, I had a "secret" garden deep in the woods, where I grew shade-loving ferns and flowering chive herbs in a pebble-lined garden surrounded by dogwood trees and winding grapevine.

I still love the unexpected and cozy feeling of outdoor dining. A regular cloth tarp hung high up in the trees can instantly become a canopy, transforming the trees into wild pillars. Comfortable pillows and blankets thrown on chairs feel even more luxurious, perhaps because they are "out of character" for being temporarily exiled outside of the home. Cocktails, summer fare, and refreshing desserts seem to taste better outdoors.

So take the party outside. Even the hottest months can be cooler outside, so just wait for the sun to set and invite friends over to dine alfresco. Toast the lazy summer nights with a glass of Prosecco, slice a rustic organic peach tart into wedges, and watch the fireflies flicker near the glowing solar lanterns. Even if you don't live near the woods, invite friends to picnic in a park. Bring an ultra-thick blanket and turn any grassy patch of land into your private dining space; let the fireflies light up the evening sky.

These ideas can turn your ho-hum BBQ into a special and elegant outdoor affair. Whether you need extra seating or a creative, last-minute dessert idea, this chapter will be a useful reference for the next time you dine under the stars.

Dine Anywhere in the Woods

It's easy to transform an outdoor dining area from too woodsy, to very cozy. A simple cloth painter's tarp borrowed from the garage can easily be recycled into a protective cover. If it's paint splattered, even better; it'll look like a hanging work of Jackson Pollock. Strong rope works best to hang the canopy high up in the trees since it will naturally fit snugly around the trees and grommets in the tarp. The table base in the photo is actually a tree stump; the dogwood tree fell down after a storm. It was cut down and leveled to 32 inches off the ground, the standard height of most dining tables. A wood top was screwed into place with four L- brackets. Lightweight wicker furniture and vintage chairs finish the dining space and throw pillows and blankets brought from indoors add comfort; upholstered tree stumps provide additional seating.

PROJECT: TREE STUMP STOOLS

Materials

Tree stumps	Hemp (or burlap)
Upholstery tacks	Hammer
Staple gun	Leftover house paint (optional)
Old cotton sweaters	Scissors
(or cotton batting)	Paintbrush

Large logs that are too big to burn in the fireplace can be transformed into charming stools. Look for logs that are level on both sides and aren't decomposing; freshly cut wood works best.

Cut the hemp fabric and cotton sweaters to size by holding a piece of fabric on top of the stump and running a pair of sharp scissors along the edge to cut out the exact shape. Staple the layers of cotton sweaters onto the top of the log (I used about 4 layers of thin cotton sweaters). Place the hemp fabric on top and, with a hammer, tack upholstery tacks all the way around. Paint the log a bright color (I used leftover house paint) or leave it unpainted to let the natural bark show through.

MOSSY TABLE SETTING

Leave the fancy floral arrangements for formal occasions and let the woodland grounds be your florist. Fill vintage candy dishes, vases, or trophies (pictured here) with moss from the woods, and poke wildflowers on top for an unexpected, elegant arrangement. Be sure to return what you've borrowed from Mother Nature back to the woods after the festivities.

Simply Green Cooking: Frozen Watermelon Martini

The freezer in my first apartment in Washington, D.C., didn't have an ice maker and I never got around to getting ice cube trays. So, on a very hot and sticky summer day—when I was entertaining a group of friends—I came up with this ice-cold and simple cocktail that was chilly, but made without any ice. Seedless watermelons work best, but regular ones will work just fine if you take care to remove the seeds while scooping out the flesh.

INGREDIENTS:

- One large, organic watermelon
- 1 or 2 ounces of vodka
- Ripe peach
- Sugar (optional)

Cut the watermelon in half. On a parchment-lined baking sheet, scoop out a single layer of watermelon balls. If you run out of room on the first baking sheet, use another. Reserve the melon rinds.

Freeze the watermelon for several hours until completely frozen. Place the frozen chunks in a blender and add 1 or 2 ounces of vodka, depending on how much watermelon is being used. Blend on the highest speed until it has a slushy consistency. Add slices of ripe peach or sugar to sweeten, if desired. Pour the cocktail into the melon bowls and serve immediately.

TERRA-COTTA
CHEESE PLATE

Whether it's a gust of wind or clumsy hands, terra-cotta pots do break, but it's no reason to throw them away. Recycle the shards into charming ID tags for your next party. They look great on a cheese plate, letting guests know what all the gourmet treats are. Either use a permanent marker to write directly onto the shards, or get crafty with a set of alphabet stamps and a permanent-ink pad, like I did here. Shards can also be used as place cards on the table.

PROJECT: GLOW-IN-THE-DARK ROCKS

Smooth river rocks and pebbles

Glow-in-the-dark paint (available at any craft store)

Foam brush

Help your guests find their way through the woods at dusk by setting a trail of glow-in-the-dark rocks. This special paint is designed to recharge throughout the day as the sun hits it, and will glow all night long once the sun sets.

Place the rocks on a newspaper-covered surface and paint thick layers of the paint on top. Let it dry completely and set a trail from the house to the outdoor dining space.

OUTDOOR LIGHTING: HANGING SOLAR LANTERNS

In addition to being very energy-efficient, solar lighting is just plain easy, too. No special wiring is needed to make solar lights work. These eco-friendly lights have built-in solar panels that power up rechargeable batteries; after a good charging in the bright sun, the built-in lights cast a soft glow all night long.

For a party, take extra precaution and put the lights in a sunny spot to charge throughout the day. After they have powered up, run a rope between trees and hang them on metal hooks above the serving table so they provide a soft glow. You can also just set them right on the table or on the ground. If you have lots of lights, make a pathway through the garden or park.

How to Choose Solar Lights

Solar lighting has improved by leaps and bounds over the years. In the past, most solar lights paled in comparison to traditional outdoor lighting; they usually emitted a very dim glow that didn't last very long, but today's solar lights cast a very strong glow.

Modern solar technology has created new outdoor lighting that is up to eighteen times brighter and shines throughout the night. In fact, it's hard to tell the difference between these lights and traditional electrical lights.

The pros of solar lamps are obvious: they don't need professional installation, they can be uprooted and moved around with ease, and they use zero electricity, which saves you money in the long run.

When shopping for solar lights, don't be tempted by the cheaper options; these are likely to be the older versions that will not meet your expectations. Instead, look for the latest versions that feature "light-emitting diodes," or LEDs, which are superbright bulbs that will last for the life of the solar light. It will cost more, but the higher price is worth it. The newer fixtures are also better designed, so despite having been made with modern technology, you can still find traditional-looking fixtures. (See resource section for retailers who sell a wide variety of solar lights).

The LED lights are common in two different forms. The most common form is path lighting. These lights come in packs and are either staked directly into the ground or hung on a metal hook. The other is task lighting, such as spotlights. These lights shine onto a specific area, like the front door or a dark corner of the yard, and are bolted directly into the home. I prefer path lighting, as I find it easier to install and has a wide variety of uses.

At my house, I use path lighting in unconventional ways, even placing the lights within branches of coniferous trees in the winter time; when the snow covers them, they still cast a pretty glow that shines through the layers of white, fluffy snow.

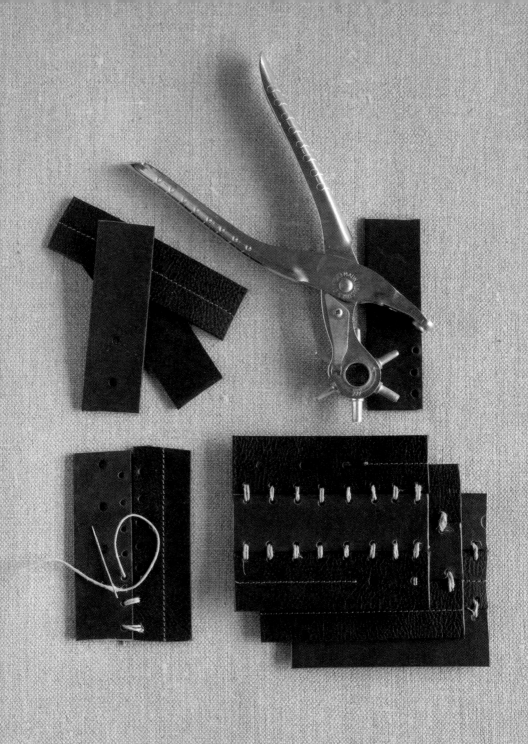

PROJECT: LEATHER-BELT COASTERS

Old leather belts can be given a new lease on life as handsome coasters. All you need to make these are a few old belts, a leather puncher, and strong, durable hemp twine. You can pick some old belts up at a local thrift shop if you don't have any to spare.

Start by cutting your old leather belts into 5-inch strips. Punch eight holes on one side of each leather strip, and punch eight holes on both sides of a single strip (this will be the center piece), all evenly spaced apart. Then thread a needle with the twine and double-stitch the leather strips together.

Tip: When shopping for used leather belts at a thrift store, remember size does count: the longer the belt, the more coasters you'll be able to make. So, shop in the men's department for the biggest belts. Also, don't pass on belts that look too worn; the finished coaster will actually look charming with a vintage appeal.

SURPRISE S'MORES TO ADORE

If you are having a cookout, you can scoop up the hot coals from the grill after you are done cooking, and surprise guests with an impromptu s'mores treat. Collect sticks from the woods or use leftover take-out Chinese chopsticks. Carefully scoop the hot coals into a fireproof dish and place on the serving table with bowls of graham crackers, exotic organic chocolate, and marshmallows. For a grown-up treat, drop organic lemon extract or peppermint essential oil onto each marshmallow for added flavor.

Using a twig or chopstick as a skewer, toast your marshmallow for a minute or two over the hot coals. Prepare an open graham-cracker-and-chocolate-bar-sandwich. Use the "sandwich" to pull your marshmallow off of the skewer. enjoy!

Organic
Wines 101

What exactly is organic wine? Basically, it is wine made from grapes that have been grown without the use of pesticides, insecticides, herbicides, and chemical fertilizers.

Conventional wine is usually made from grapes that have been sprayed with some or all of the above. This is the cheapest and easiest way for growers to protect their crops from disease, weeds, and insect infestations. It's easy to spot a non-organic vineyard. A drive through Napa Valley in California will reveal mostly gorgeous vineyards with grapevines that have vibrantly green leaves and plump grapes, all in perfect rows without a weed in sight. The more perfect-looking the vineyard, the more chemicals have probably been used. In this case, aesthetics do not rule. A typical organic vineyard isn't so picture perfect, with cover crops growing in between wild-looking vines. But make no mistake about it: prettier doesn't mean better tasting.

One of the main reasons to choose organic wines is that the residue from the chemicals has the potential to end up in the wine itself, when the grapes are pressed and put into vats. Also, organic wines have fewer sulfites (a preservative) in them. While it is a misconception that organic wines do not have any sulfites, they do have less than conventional wines. During the fermentation process, all wines will develop naturally occurring sulfites, but most organic vineyards will stop there and do not add additional preservatives. This can be a blessing for wine lovers. Many people who claim to get headaches from wine—especially red wine—often say they do not suffer the same problem from organic wines due to the lower sulfite content.

Organic wines are often some of the best wines, too. Since most vintners pay impeccable detail to their vines, such as amending the soil by hand, the attention often leads to better quality and often award-winning wines. Frog's Leap, one of my favorite California wineries, has always been organic, and its impressive list of wines has consistently been awarded glowing reviews.

On your next visit to the wine store, ask about organic options; you'll be surprised at the number of varietals available to you.

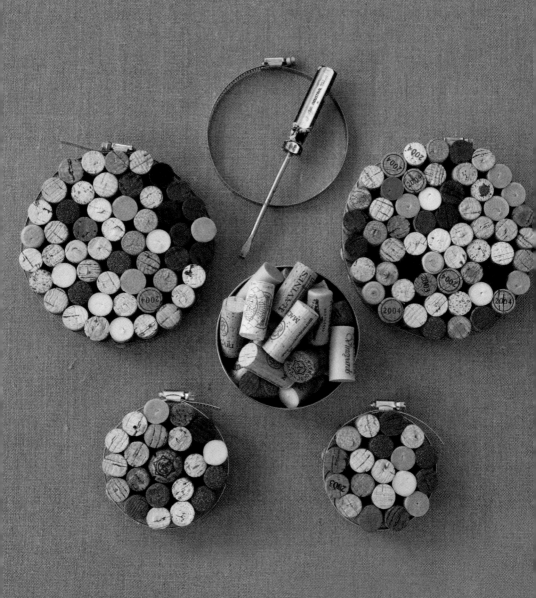

PROJECT: CORK TRIVET

Materials

Approximately 50 corks

A 6- or 7-inch round metal pipe clamp
   (available at any hardware store)

Screwdriver

Here's a great use for all those wine and champagne corks you may have been storing in the kitchen drawer. Recycle them into a useful and decorative cork trivet to help protect your kitchen and tabletop surfaces. This project will work with both real and synthetic corks. If you don't have enough corks, check with your local restaurant, bar, or wine store to see if they can save corks for you. I've discovered these places are usually more than happy to give them to you for free, especially if you are a regular customer.

Arrange the corks inside the pipe clamp in a tight, uniform pattern. Make sure the pipe clamp is centered on the sides of the corks and tighten with a screwdriver until the corks are completely snug.

Tip: If you want to remove any of the red-wine stains from the cork, simply soak them in a bowl of water with a little bleach overnight. Rinse them clean and let them dry thoroughly before making the trivet.

A BABY
SHOWER

When a good friend announced she was expecting, I immediately began planning a baby shower for her. As a gift, I wanted to handle all the details. The thing that really made the party spark was that the ratio of guys to girls was much higher. The untraditional guest list included her friends and family, her husband's friends, and friends of her family.

I made the invitations by hand, and figured out a creative way to use very inexpensive, used baby clothes from Goodwill or the Salvation Army as invitations. The end result was a big hit with the guests. The day before the shower, the rented chairs, tables, and tents were placed in the middle of a meadow, dotted with wildflowers and an unusually high number of four-leaf clovers (a good sign!). A small pile of freshly ironed red bandannas became napkins and were stacked neatly on top of bamboo plates and biodegradable cutlery made entirely from sugarcane. Even though fine china and metal utensils would be the most ecological, I didn't feel guilty at all by using these eco-disposables.

Complementing the perfect spring day I served curried organic egg-salad sandwiches on thick slices of homemade Amish breads, and soy "chicken" salad sandwiches

with crunchy celery bits and cilantro that were wrapped in simple but rustic waxed paper, tied with red-and-white bakery string. Freshly baked cookies and snow cones satisfied everyone's sweet tooth.

As guests left, I offered each a burlap-wrapped baby tree complete with a note reading, "As Tiffany's son grows up, so will this tree, helping to ensure a cleaner, brighter and better future for him. Here's to you, my friend, and your son, Davin."

This section includes all of these projects, plus a few more fun surprises, to help you throw a special shower or party for a friend.

Red-and-White Table Setting

Renting party items is a nice ecological option to buying disposable goods or items that will only be used once and then stuffed in a closet. Unfortunately, in most small towns the choice in tables, chairs, and tents from rental companies can be very limited. I remember going to my local store and asking, "Do you have Moroccan silk tents?" and the confused store owner's reply was, "We have *a* tent, the one you see right in front of you." The simplest solution is to stick to one color scheme: white. Most rental stores will have white chairs, white tables, and white tents, and collectively they provide a simple look that can be dressed up with doses of color.

For the baby shower, the color scheme was red and white: Red seat cushions were borrowed from friends, raw hemp fabric was dyed a vivid ruby to protect the table's surface, and red bandannas were tied with red string and became napkins. Glass jars were filled with citronella wax to keep mosquitoes at bay, and small dishes of white candy were scattered for guests to nibble on.

But even this color rule was meant to be broken: If you don't have red or white flowers, cut young tree branches for your centerpieces. Since lilac bushes were in full bloom during the shower, I put them in a mix of glass vases and bottles and placed them down the center of the table. The fragrance from their blooms more than compensated for breaking up the color scheme.

PROJECT: BABY-CLOTHES
SHOWER INVITATIONS

100% cotton baby clothes
  (from Goodwill or a thrift shop)
Iron-on transfer paper
  (from any office-supply store)
Iron
Ribbon

Here's a resourceful twist to a baby shower invitation. Pick up inexpensive, slightly worn baby clothes from Goodwill or any thrift shop. Be sure to read the labels carefully and purchase only 100 percent cotton clothing since transfer paper works best on it.

On a computer, type out the event details of the baby shower using a simple, easy-to-read font. Be efficient and maximize the number of invites per page to reduce waste. Print the invites on the iron-on transfer paper; be sure to print the invites in "mirror image" mode. After printing, neatly cut out the invite details, cutting as close to the words as possible.

Using an iron on the hottest setting (with no steam), iron the paper (print side down) onto the baby clothes with a few, firm swipes of the iron. Allow to cool completely and peel off the backing paper. Roll up and tie with a ribbon.

Baby Shower!

Please join us in honor of
Tiffany Sondergaard

Sunday, May 15th
Noon, Sharp

Hosted by Danny Seo

Tiffany is registered at Babies R Us

Keep details and directions attached.

Baby Shower!

Please join us in honor of
Tiffany Sondergaard

by Danny Seo

registered at Babies R Us

details and directions attached.

Baby Shower!

Please join us in honor of
Tiffany Sondergaard

Sunday, May 15th
Noon, Sharp

Hosted by Danny Seo

Tiffany is registered at Babies R Us

Keep details and directions attached.

HEALTHY SNOW CONES

Snow cones bring back memories of warm-weather treats. But today's shaved ices are often doused in unhealthy sugary syrups full of artificial colors and flavors. Here's a delicious alternative that will keep both kids and kids-at-heart happy.

You can rent a professional snow-cone machine for very little money from the same store you rented the party fixtures; they usually come equipped with scoops and paper cones, too. All you need is ice and a selection of juices to flavor them. Try antioxidant-rich pomegranate (pictured) or cranberry juice. If you like, you can also try vitamin-fortified waters or sports drinks for an electrolyte-fueled treat.

Simply Green Cooking: Herb Salad with Ricotta Dressing

I used to eat this salad five times a week. I love the distinctive taste of ginger in the dressing. While nothing beats the freshness of baby spring lettuce right from the garden or farmer's market, a good timesaver is the pre-washed, herb-blend organic salad mixes from companies like Earthbound Farms and Fresh Express.

INGREDIENTS:

4 tablespoons of extra-virgin olive oil
   (about three swirls in a large mixing bowl)

2 tablespoons of good balsamic vinegar

½ cup of whole-milk ricotta cheese

1 tablespoon of Dijon mustard

1 tablespoon of honey (about one good squeeze from the bottle)

1 tablespoon of freshly grated ginger (I use a pre-minced,
   jarred ginger from The Ginger People)

Pinch of kosher salt

Fresh ground pepper

Dill (optional)

Mixed greens

Start by whisking the olive oil and balsamic vinegar together in a large mixing bowl until emulsified. Add the ricotta cheese, mustard, honey, ginger, salt, and pepper and whisk together. Toss with the washed mixed greens and serve. If you use only baby greens for the salad, add fresh dill to the salad for an extra-savory herb flavor.

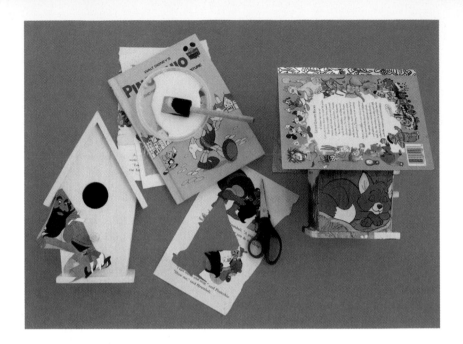

PROJECT: STORYBOOK BIRDHOUSE PROJECT

Materials

Unfinished wood birdhouse

Children's hardcover storybook

Staple gun

Scissors

Foam brush

Decoupage glue (like Mod Podge)

Varnish (optional)

A handmade gift is a wonderful way to show you care. This simple project transforms an ordinary, unpainted wood birdhouse (from any craft store) into something almost magical—a perfect decorative touch for any nursery.

First, choose a children's story book that is large enough to fold over the roof of the birdhouse, and cover it completely. Remove all the pages from inside the book and set aside. Staple the book directly onto the roof; placing one staple on the left and one on the right side of the roof should hold it.

Using a pair of scissors, trim the pages of the book to fit along the sides of the birdhouse. Generously brush on the decoupage glue to adhere the paper to the birdhouse and then use additional glue on top; it will dry clear and create a protective coating. Overlap pages until the entire house is covered. Let it dry completely. To make it waterproof for outdoor use, you can add a layer of varnish onto the finished birdhouse.

PROJECT: CHOPSTICK COASTERS

Take-out Chinese chopsticks

Gardening shears

Cordless drill

$^5/_{64}$-inch drill bit

Needle

String

Glass beads

These elegant coasters are actually made from something found in most people's junk drawers: take-out Chinese chopsticks.

Using sharp gardening shears, cut each chopstick exactly in half. Using a $^5/_{64}$-inch bit, drill a hole approximately ½ inch from the top and bottom of each chopstick.

Thread a needle with a double-strand of string, run it through the top hole of one chopstick, and make a knot at the end large enough so it will not slip through the hole. Add a glass bead or two, then another chopstick, then another bead, and continue until you reach the desired size. Repeat the process on the bottom ends of the chopsticks. Leave the excess string for a decorative touch.

Tip: For extra-strong chopstick coasters, consider using dental floss instead of string. Also, a good place to find stray Chinese food take-out chopsticks is at your office; your colleagues probably have a pile of them stashed away in their desk drawer that they'd be happy to give to you.

Seven Tips to Turn Any Caterer Organic

Finding a good caterer on a budget can be a real challenge, but finding a purely organic caterer can seem impossible. However, it's easy to work with any caterer to create delicious appetizers, meals, and desserts that are also healthy and earth friendly.

Tip 1: Ask for easy-to-find organic staples like sugar, eggs, milk, butter, and spices. Since many of these ingredients are comparable in price to conventional ones and are easy to find, it shouldn't affect the bottom line.

Tip 2: Use local ingredients. Visit your local farmer's market and see what's in season. In Pennsylvania, tomatoes are in a great abundance near the end of summer; it's almost impossible for farmers to give them away! Having the caterer whip up a fresh, organic gazpacho would be a nice choice for a summertime starter.

Tip 3: Offer to pay a little more. In the food services business, a dollar here and a dollar there adds up on the bottom line over time; the profit margins for most caterers are so slim that they try to use the least expensive ingredients. If you offer to pay a little more for the food, they may be willing to source organically for you.

Tip 4: Use your own serving dishes, platters, and trays. Instead of packing the food in disposable plastic and Styrofoam containers, ask the caterer to use your own serving pieces. Not only will you cut down on waste, but you'll save time by not having to transfer the food.

Tip 5: Leave the disposables behind. Many caterers will include disposable utensils, napkins, cups, and straws. Opt to use your own reusable ones or rentals, and inform the caterer ahead of time so they can be kept out of your order. You may even get a small discount.

Tip 6: Don't be afraid to ask for a healthier version of a dish. For the baby shower, I asked for mostly egg-white, curried salad. I compensated for the missing yolks by adding crunchy sprouts and vegetables into the low-cholesterol, egg-salad sandwiches. I also offered to make and wrap the sandwiches myself, which dramatically cut down on the price. Pictured are the wrapped sandwiches in earth-friendly wax paper and tied with colorful red-and-white bakery string.

Tip 7: If the caterer will also be providing a coffee and tea service, insist on organic, shade-grown coffee and a selection of organic teas. These are easily sourced items. Keep the creamers off the caterer's to-do list and provide your own organic creamer, fat-free milk, and soy milk for guests. Fill a pretty bowl with some of your own natural or organic sugar straight from the pantry.

PROJECT: ORGANIC BABY-CLOTHES CUSTOMIZATION STATION

Keeping guests engaged at a party is a great icebreaker, and makes everyone feel welcome. At this untraditional baby shower, both men and women were invited, so I came up with an activity they'd all enjoy.

For very little money, I purchased a selection of undyed, very basic organic baby clothes from an online retailer. The onesies, T-shirts, pajama bottoms, and even a few receiving blankets were just begging to be embellished.

To create your own baby-clothes customization station, be sure to have enough items so that each guest can customize one article of clothing with a special design. All you need is a selection of permanent fabric markers and your guests' imaginations. Hang up a clothesline and display the finished creations so other guests can admire the decorated wardrobe. At the end of the shower, fold up all the clothes and place them in a wicker basket with a bottle of gentle, eco-friendly detergent like Method Home: a very personal and useful gift for the mom-to-be.

PROJECT: BABY TREE THANK-YOU GIFTS

Here's a thoughtful way to say thank you to guests for attending the baby shower: a baby tree. Purchase young, easy-to-carry coniferous or deciduous trees from a local nursery. Clip off the growing instructions and set aside. Wrap the plastic container in layers of burlap and tie with a pretty ribbon. Tie on a large manila hangtag (from the office-supply store) with a handwritten note and tape the growing instructions on the reverse side.

How to
Plant a Tree

Many non-gardeners find the idea of planting a live tree daunting. In reality, even for the novice gardener, planting trees is one of the easiest things to do.

The rule of thumb is to plant trees in their ideal growing area. Read the growing instructions that come with the tree carefully. If it calls for a sunny area, scan your property for a site that gets direct sun for most of the day. Likewise, if it calls for a shady spot, look for an area that is protected from the sun.

Once you pick a spot, dig a whole twice as wide as the root ball, or container. The hole should be just about the same height of the container. Save the soil you dig out, since you'll use that to fill in the hole after the tree is planted.

Unroot the tree from the container and place it in the hole and fill it with soil. The soil should be firmly placed, but not packed in. After filling in the hole, cover it with an eco-friendly mulch like cocoa-bean hulls; this mulch is made from the actual shells of cocoa beans and has a strong chocolate scent. When wet, the shells "gel" together and form a protective mat that keeps weeds out, but lets water and air in.

Water the tree thoroughly, as this will help it settle. Check daily for the first week and touch the soil. If it feels wet, don't water it, but if it feels dry, give it a good soak.

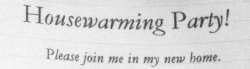

Housewarming Party!

Please join me in my new home.

Wednesday, October 7th

7:00 PM

Please bring an unwanted (yet stylish)
vase, lamp, bowl, blanket and more
for a fun recycling swap.

(Directions & Address on back.)

See you then!

Danny Seo

Party 3

A HOUSEWARMING

When I moved into my new house, I threw a party that was a little different. Since there are no real traditions in throwing a housewarming bash, I wanted to create some of my own. I decided to use materials that are normally left over from any big move or restoration. Tile from a bathroom renovation job, sandpaper, wallpaper swatch books, and paint chips were all recycled into useful and fun accessories for the party.

I asked my guests not to bring presents, except for wine. You can never have enough wine at a party! Instead, I had them bring something they no longer wanted, but was still useful: a vase, a lamp, a sculpture, a collection of antique books. Come with a mirror, leave with a set of shot glasses! And we turned the night into a swap party.

And even though I asked my guests not to bring gifts to my own housewarming, I love bringing special gifts to my friends' parties. My favorite housewarming gift is an assortment of Chinese coins and precious metal beads that are strung on a silk string and then hung by the door; the coins are believed to bring good luck.

While these ideas are the culmination of a few housewarming parties I've thrown, they can be used for any special event you put together.

Sandpaper Housewarming Invite

Here's a clever way to recycle leftover sandpaper into a charming housewarming invitation.

Print the details of the party on an interesting paper. I used inexpensive graph paper and printed four invitations on each sheet. Cut the invitation to size and attach it to a sheet of sandpaper by punching two small holes at the top and threading a piece of string through them; hemp twine works well.

The invitation will fit in a standard A2 envelope, which is 4⅜ by 5¾ inches, and available at any office-supply store. If you choose to mail them, be sure to add the appropriate postage; sandpaper can vary in weight and affect the postage.

OPEN HOUSE, OPEN TEA BAR

This is a zen-like approach to a wet bar: a do-it-yourself tea bar.

I used this antique Korean apothecary stand, but you can offer out a selection of dried teas in pretty bowls or tins. Set out plenty of teacups and saucers, individual tea strainers, and spoons for guests to scoop teas and stir their own drinks; make sure to have plenty of organic lemon wedges and wild honey on hand.

Encourage guests to mix their own custom blends. I set out a selection of organic teas including English breakfast, chamomile, jasmine, mint, and a citrus zinger. To help guests identify which tea is which, try recycling laminate card samples into ID tags; these faux wood laminate cards are potential countertop options from a kitchen improvement store. I used a set of alphabet stamps and a permanent-ink pad to stamp each the name of tea onto a card and hung them with hemp string.

PROJECT: TEA TIN VASES

Materials

Decorative tea tins

Cordless drill

⁹⁄₆₄-inch drill bit

Four matching cabinet knobs

Candle

Cut flowers (such as inexpensive carnations)

You can recycle empty tea tins into something pretty and useful. If you are an avid tea drinker, this is a great way to amass a collection of one-of-a-kind vases.

Drill a hole in each corner of the bottom of the tea tin. Screw the cabinet knobs into the holes so they are snug against the bottom of the tin. Light a candle and let wax drip inside the tin, making sure the hot wax collects around the holes where you previously drilled. This will ensure that the tin is waterproof.

Vibrant-colored flowers look best in these tins; I filled these with inexpensive carnations from the supermarket. When tightly grouped together, the carnations take on an elegant and bountiful appearance.

Simply Green Cooking: Easy Housewarming Appetizers

. . . .

The overwhelming amount of work one does when moving into a new home can leave very little time to cook up a feast for a housewarming. The trick to keeping guests happy and yourself sane is to offer a small variety of good-quality beverages and bite-sized treats. Offer your guests familiar foods with an unexpected twist. Save time by buying store-bought and frozen-food items for the party. With a little embellishment, even the simplest heat-and-serve snack can be a gourmet treat.

- Pick up a cheese pizza from your favorite pizzeria. Cut it up into bite-sized squares with a sharp knife (or use a cookie cutter in a pretty shape) and sprinkle with finely chopped fresh herbs like cilantro or dill. Dollop trout caviar, which is a sustainable choice, on top of each piece. (Most good caviar is from sturgeon from the Caspian Sea, and their populations have been dwindling due to overfishing; avoid this type of caviar and choose a variety that is domestically sourced in the United States.) If desired, add a dollop of crème fraiche on top.

- Stuff ripe, sweet figs with a spoonful of tangy goat cheese, and drizzle wild honey on top. Serve on a tray with a small bowl of bamboo skewers on the side so guests can easily pick them up and pop them in their mouth.

- Buy good, hand-cut French fries from a local burger joint and keep them warm in the oven. Sprinkle with finely chopped parsley and drizzle with fragrant truffle oil. Serve in individual dishes or brown paper lunch bags so guests can nibble on their own serving of fries. Try drizzling truffle oil on freshly popped organic microwave popcorn, too.

- Fill organic endive leaves with crumbled blue cheese and top with a dollop of mango chutney.

- Boil frozen vegetarian dumplings and place each one on an oversized soupspoon. Drizzle sesame oil and sprinkle toasted sesame seeds on top and garnish each dumpling with one cilantro leaf. Guests can pick up the spoons and pop the dumplings in their mouths.

PROJECT: BLUEPRINT TABLE RUNNER

After a new home is finished, most homeowners stash the blueprints away never to be seen again. Instead of filing them, recycle your blueprints into a durable and attractive tablecloth. I transformed a blueprint into a runner, pictured here, which is protecting my antique podium table. If you don't happen to have a blueprint, you can find ones at garage sales and online at auction sites like eBay.

Any office-supply store can professionally laminate your blueprints for very little money; after they're sealed, you can cut them to any size you like. Consider making a long table runner or keep it large enough to cover a square or rectangular dining table. Any leftover blueprint paper can be cut down and made into hardworking, everyday placemats.

PLEASE
HELP
YOURSELF!

SOCKS AT THE FRONT DOOR

In many Asian countries, it is customary to remove your shoes at the door before entering one's house. And for good reason: Most household dirt is carried in by your shoes.

If you ask guests to remove their shoes at your next event, consider this fun and inviting option. Provide a bowl of clean, new wool and cashmere socks they can wear after removing their shoes. A sporting goods store is a great place to find inexpensive wool fishing socks. Have a variety of sizes on hand for both men and women; if children are invited, be sure to have children's socks, too. If you are so inclined, offer guests the option of keeping the socks as a thank-you gift.

As an added gesture, have rolled-up newspaper on hand and gently insert it into their shoes; throughout the party, the newspaper will detoxify their shoes by absorbing excess moisture and odor.

Simple Ways to Detox Your Home

A clean house is more than just sparkling countertops and well-vacuumed floors; it's fresh-smelling and chemical-free too. Here are some Simply Green ways to detox your home:

- Instead of using a synthetic air freshener to get rid of a smell, open a window or use an exhaust fan instead. Aerosol air fresheners emit volatile organic compounds into the air, which can irritate your eyes and lead to headaches.

- If your refrigerator has a drip pan, clean it out every month. The moisture in the pan can breed mold and other bacteria.

- Use nontoxic cleaning supplies. Eco-friendly, all-purpose cleaners can now be easily found at major discount retailers and supermarket chains. Their effectiveness has improved and prices have come down. To make cleaning even more appealing, add a few drops of essential oil to the bottle. While you clean, you'll fill the room with a fresh, natural scent.

- If you have central air conditioning, wipe down the vents where the air comes out. The dust that collects on the vents could recirculate when the air flows out.

- Lose the vinyl shower curtain. Most shower curtains (including all liners) are polyvinyl chloride (PVC)–based, which release chemical odors and gases into your house almost the second they are taken out of their packaging. They can continue to release these gases for years. A simple solution is to take a cue from hotel chains: Go nylon. These simple, white nylon shower curtains do not need a liner and are easy to clean; just unhook and throw into the washing machine. Good as new!

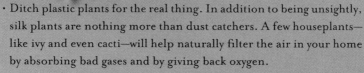

- Ditch plastic plants for the real thing. In addition to being unsightly, silk plants are nothing more than dust catchers. A few houseplants—like ivy and even cacti—will help naturally filter the air in your home by absorbing bad gases and by giving back oxygen.

- Microwave sponges. After washing the dishes, toss the wet sponge into the microwave and nuke it on high for about a minute. This will radiate all the bacteria away and make sure it's germ-free the next time you use it.

47

HOUSEWARMING GIFT SWAP

This idea goes all the way back to my twelfth birthday party, when I asked my friends to keep their gifts and instead donate their time to environmental activism. In the spirit of recycling, engage your guests in a home-décor gift swap.

Ask guests to bring one household item that is desirable, functional, and stylish that they no longer have a use for; a set of antique dishes, a table lamp, a serving tray, bookends, candlesticks, and framed artwork are good ideas. That means, no DVD players or exercise equipment!

Gather all the items together and have everyone put their name in a bowl. Mix up the names and pull them out one at a time. When a name is called, that person can choose an item from the gift pile as their own. To make things even more interesting, have several "mystery" boxes on hand; put some of your own treasured items into the mystery boxes and one or two gift certificates to a home-furnishings store.

If there are any items left over at the end of the swap, pack them up and donate them to Goodwill or the Salvation Army.

Tip: Try a gift-swap party for other celebrations as well. Exchange baby clothes at a baby shower in a room full of moms or unwanted jewelry at a bachelorette party. The number of "theme" swap-party possibilities is endless.

PROJECT: WINEGLASS ID TAGS

Materials

Paint chip cards

1-inch hole puncher

¼-inch hole puncher

½ to 1-inch ring clips (from any office-supply store)

Permanent marker

Choosing a paint color can be an overwhelming decision, which often leads to stacks of paint chips. Recycle them into useful ID tags for wineglasses. This is a simple and easy way to help guests keep track of their stemware.

Use the 1-inch hole punch to cut out round circles from the paint chips; try to cut as many circles as possible from each card to minimize waste.

Punch a ¼-inch hole at the top of the circle and attach a ring clip that fits snugly around the stem of the wineglass.

As guests take their first glass of wine, write their name onto the chip with a permanent marker.

Tip: Accidents do happen, so if a guest spills red wine all over your white shag carpet, don't freak out. Neutralize it by sprinkling the red wine stain with white wine; it acts like a bleach and magically removes the stain.

51

PROJECT: PAINT-CHIP PLACE CARDS

Clearly, I'm a little obsessed with finding myriad uses for the simple paint chip. Here's another: Use it as a simple, yet colorful and effective, place card. To begin, run a sharp kitchen knife through the top of a champagne cork and slowly make an incision about one-third of the way down. If the cork doesn't stand upright on its own, shave a little off the bottom until it is level.

Insert a paint chip and write your guest's name as a place card or, as I've done here, place them by cocktail snacks to help guests know what they're eating.

PROJECT: HARDWOOD TRAY

When building a new home, flooring companies will often give you sample pieces of wood flooring to help you visualize how the floors would look in your home. You can also purchase a piece of plywood at a home-improvement or hardware store or use the top of a small wooden table instead. It's surprisingly easy to recycle these handsome wood boards into hardworking serving trays.

Search garage sales or salvage stores for decorative handles. The handles I've used were originally from a local church. Look for a matching pair and make sure they are big enough that your hands can grasp them comfortably; this will ensure the finished tray will be easy for you to carry.

Screw the handles into the board; use matching screws to complete the elegant look. The finished tray can also be a portable cutting board for slicing bread and cheese.

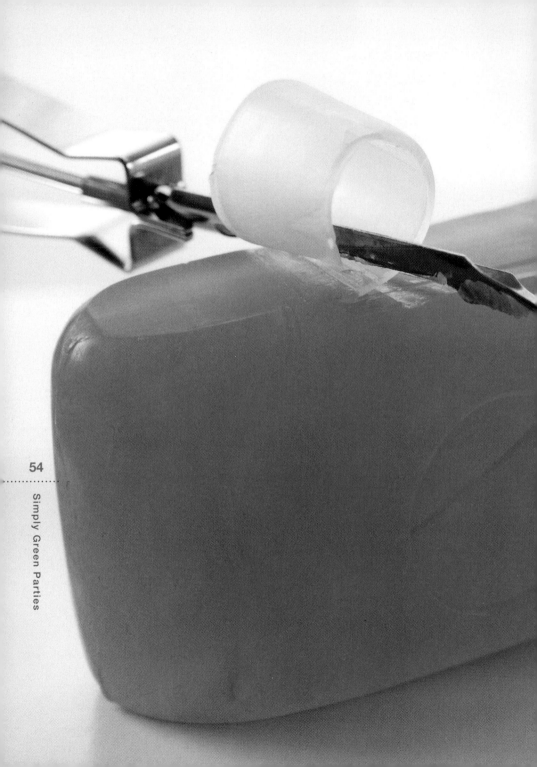

PROJECT: SINGLE-USE SOAP PETALS

Here's an unexpected gesture of kindness for guests: individual soap curls.

Simply run a vegetable peeler across the top of a bar of glycerin soap. The peeler will shave off thin strips of soap, which will naturally form into a pretty curl. Fill a decorative bowl with the soap curls and place it by the sink; each curl should be just enough soap for an individual hand-washing.

Materials

Ceramic tile

Rubbing alcohol

Cotton balls

Porcelain paint

Foam brush

Wood-graining tool (found at any hardware store)

Rag

Felt-pad stickers

Any ceramic tile can become a useful trivet or coaster in the kitchen to protect surfaces from damage. Here's a stylish way to turn leftover tile into a beautiful and useful accompaniment. With a cotton ball, wipe the tile clean with the rubbing alcohol and allow it to dry completely; the alcohol will help bond the paint to the tile's surface. Paint a coat of the porcelain paint using the foam brush. Run the wood-graining tool across the top while the paint is still wet to create a faux finish. Wipe the graining tool clean with a rag. Allow to dry (about 30 minutes).

Place the tile in a cold oven and heat it for 20 minutes at 350 degrees; turn off the oven and let the tile cool completely inside the oven. Once cool, attach felt-pad stickers on the reverse side.

A set of wood-grained coasters also makes a lovely housewarming gift.

Tip: Try glass paint on glass tiles with the same wood-graining technique for an ethereal look.

Party 4

HAPPY
BIRTHDAY

One of the great things about birthdays is that at any age, you can still be young at heart when celebrating. I love giving activities associated with children's parties a grown-up twist, like an "adult piñata." Instead of candy, my piñata is filled with grown-up goodies like small spa amenities, mini liquor bottles, and gift cards.

I put this party together in the garden of my longtime public relations manager, Claudine Gumbel, at her New York City garden apartment she shares with her husband, Brian. I hope you'll see some fun and easy ideas you can use at your next bash. The event was grown-up (champagne and organic wine flowed freely), but young, too (cupcakes, cakes, cookies, and lots of candles)—a wonderful combination.

Edible Pastry Leaves

Photo cakes are a familiar sight at many supermarket bakeries; you bring in a photo of a loved one, and the bakery will transfer the image onto a cake. But your family photos aren't the only images you can transfer.

Collect colorful leaves from your yard and bring them to the bakery. The bakery will place them on a computer scanner, and the images of the leaves will be transferred onto an 8½-by-11-inch edible pastry sheet printed with edible inks. Cut out the leaves with a pair of cuticle scissors. Place the edible leaves on top of cupcakes (pictured here) or on a simple, frosted cake. Also try fern fronds, sticks, and flowers.

Simply Green Cooking:
Quick Sweet Treats

A birthday dinner party doesn't always have to end with cake and ice cream. Here are a few last-minute treats that will keep your guests' sweet tooth satisfied and happy.

- Dip extra-thick potato chips (look for locally made ones or brand-name organic ones seasoned with sea salt) in dark, melted chocolate; after dipping, cool on a parchment-lined baking sheet and chill in the refridgerator until set. You can also use store-bought organic pretzels. Either way, the saltiness and sugar come together to create one savory and sweet satisfying crunch.

- Try a simple Italian treat called affogato: brew organic coffee extra strong in the coffeemaker. Scoop vanilla ice cream into bowls and pour some coffee on top. For an extra indulgence, add slivers of candied ginger. Serve immediately.

- If it's summertime, gather everyone in the car and head to a pick-your-own berry farm; if it's organic, even better. Pack a cooler with ice, a carton of whipping cream, a metal bowl, honey, a whisk, and some bamboo skewers. While everyone is off picking berries, whip up some cream with honey; let everyone dip their berries on skewers in the whipped cream for an instant, fresh-off-the-vine goodness treat.

- If you don't have time to heat up the grill, pull out that infomercial splurge: the George Foreman grill. Slice peaches in half and grill, flesh side down. Serve the warm peaches with vanilla ice cream and crumble vanilla cookies on top.

- During the holiday season, this is a tasty way to recycle candy. Throw a few candy canes into the blender and pulverize them into a minty, powdered sugar. Spike them with homemade hot chocolate with it and add another peppermint stick to garnish. If you have chocolate candies, too, add one to the bottom of each mug for a sweet treat after the cocoa is all gone.

PROJECT: TRIFLE-DISH CANDLEHOLDER

Trifle desserts have been around since the sixteenth century. Originally made from leftover bread sweetened with layers of sugar, cream, rosewater, and liquor, today's trifles seem to have become an unappetizing mess. I've even seen some with nondairy whipped topping, canned fruit, and stale store-bought cookies. Yuck!

But even if the trifle's best days are in the past, glass trifle stands still have good times ahead of them. These stands can be easily found for a song at thrift shops and flea markets. An elegant way to recycle them is to transform them into a candleholder. Simply purchase four individual glass candleholders from a home-décor store; insert white candles and place inside the trifle dish. The candles will burn inside the dish and cast a romantic glow throughout the room

PROJECT: BROWN-PAPER-BAG BIRTHDAY LANTERNS

Brown-paper shopping bags of different sizes

3-inch alphabet stencil kit (from any office-supply store)

Scissors

Double-stick tape

Tissue paper

Kitty litter, pebbles, or sand

Rechargeable or tea-light candles (optional)

What a festive way to greet your guests—glowing luminaires reading, "HAPPY BIRTHDAY!" This is a resourceful way of recycling boring brown-paper shopping bags into something pretty and handmade. Don't worry if they don't exactly match. They will still look great.

To begin, trace the stencils with a pencil on the paper bags, fitting as many letters across each bag as possible to spell out HAPPY BIRTHDAY. With a pair of sharp scissors, cut out each letter on the front side of the bag, being careful not to accidentally poke through the back side. After cutting out all the letters, use double-stick tape to attach colorful tissue paper inside the bag.

To illuminate the bags, weigh them down with kitty litter, pebbles, or sand. Insert a rechargeable candle inside each bag, or light a tea-light candle protected by a glass holder. Experiment with different bags, tissue paper, and stencils and create luminaires for other events, too, like New Year's Eve and anniversary parties.

PROJECT: RECYCLED COMPACT INVITATIONS

Materials

Used makeup compacts, thoroughly cleaned

2-inch hole puncher

Decorative paper

Double-stick tape or glue

Grosgrain ribbon

For a change from the store-bought or e-mail invitations, try these pretty invitations that are literally compact. If you don't have compacts, a collection of ring boxes would work well, too.

Using the hole puncher, punch out circles from a pretty remnant paper, like wrapping paper, and glue the circles inside the compacts, both top and bottom. Attach a 6-inch piece of matching grosgrain ribbon with tape or glue to the inside of the compact and glue a photo of the guest of honor and party details to the ribbon. Fold the ribbon upon itself and close the compact shut.

Tip: To clean the compacts thoroughly, use very hot water in the kitchen sink to literally melt the makeup away. Scrub any remaining makeup with dish soap and a sponge, and use a cotton towel to dry them.

PROJECT: SOLID PERFUME CARRYING CASES

Used makeup compacts, thoroughly cleaned

¼ cup of solid beeswax

3 tablespoons of jojoba oil

Approximately 60 drops of essential oil

Pyrex measuring cup

For a thoughtful and fragrant last-minute gift, a compact can also be turned into a solid perfume carrying case. This would make an especially nice gift for a bachelorette party or shower.

Begin by melting the beeswax in a Pyrex measuring cup in the microwave. Add the jojoba oil (which will prvent the perfume from going rancid) and the essential oil. Stir the mixture and pour into the compacts; allow to cool completely. To use, simply dab your fingers over the wax and apply.

Tip: This can be a fun DIY project at a party, too. Have a number of essential oils on hand—rose, lavender, chamomile—and let guests customize their own solid perfume scents.

69

BIRDBATH WINE COOLER

A birdbath gives our feathered friends a source of fresh water to quench their thirst; it can also be used to chill wines and champagne to help quench *our* thirst.

Simply fill the birdbath with ice and add bottles of white and sparkling wines.

PROJECT: SPA PIÑATA

Balloon	Prizes (see below)
Newspaper	Hole puncher
Scissors	Twine
White craft glue	Tape
Foam Brush	Leaves

What could be more fun than a piñata at a party? This is a grown-up twist on the childhood tradition: a spa piñata full of feel-good treats any grown-up would want to have.

Start by blowing up a large balloon. Cut newspaper into long strips and coat each side with slightly watered-down white glue. Cover the whole balloon with the newspaper strips and allow to dry for a few hours. Repeat the process until you have three or four layers. Dry overnight.

Cut a 3-inch square into the piñata, but leave one side uncut so it works as a flap. Discard the popped balloon. Fill with grown-up goodies like single-use foot- and hand-scrubs, travel-sized lotions, lip balm, pumice stones, granola bars, and music download gift cards. For a more guy-themed party, add lottery tickets, tins of peppermints, and even small action figures.

Using a hole puncher, make two holes wherever you decide the top is and run a piece of strong twine between the holes; this will allow you to hang up the piñata. Tape the square flap back into place and glue large leaves all over the piñata. Hang from a tree and be sure to let the birthday guest of honor take the first swing.

PROJECT: TREASURE CANDLES

Metal or stone charms, gemstones, or coins (no plastic)

Microwaveable soy candle wax (available at any craft store)

Pyrex measuring cup

Crayon remnants (optional)

Pre-tabbed candlewicks, approximately 5 to 8 inches in length
  (available at any craft store)

Waxy cardboard juice or milk containers or
  fireproof glass containers

Scissors

Recycle old charms, semiprecious gemstones, and vintage Cracker Jack prizes into a handmade treasure candle. Use a microwaveable soy candle wax to create the candles. Melt the wax according to package instructions in a Pyrex measuring cup in the microwave and, if desired, add crayon remnants to dye the wax. Secure the pre-tabbed candlewick in the center of the mold or glass container. Carefully fill halfway with melted wax; let it cool completely. Add two or three treasures and fill with remaining wax and allow to cool; do not add any treasures that are made of plastic, since they will melt. Trim wicks. To remove treasures from a burning candle, use tweezers to protect fingers from the flame.

Tip: You can find vintage charms at most flea markets and antique stores. They are usually sold as a lot, meaning that there will be a variety of charms sold together for one price. This is not only an economical way to purchase vintage charms, but can be a lot of fun, too. You never know what you're going to get.

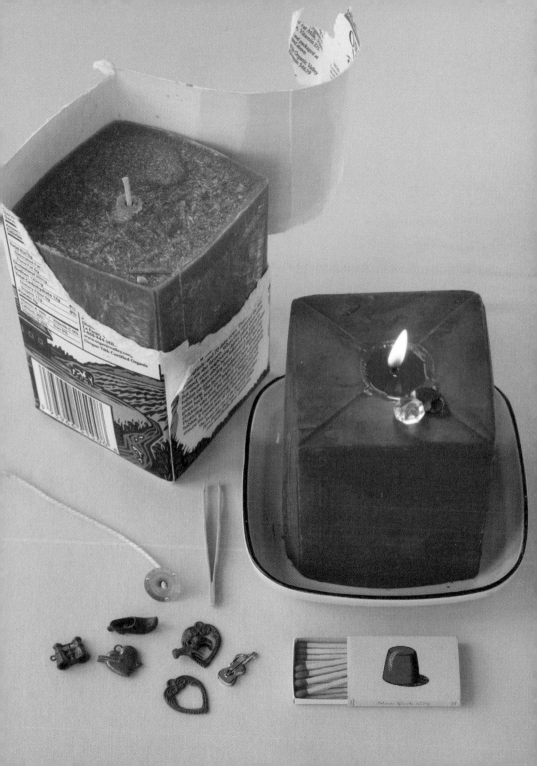

Choosing Eco-friendly Candles

At your next event, try an environmentally friendly alternative to traditional candles. Most candles are made from paraffin wax, which is petroleum-based. When these candles are lit, they emit soot and other air toxins into your home. If you've ever burned a candle too close to a wall and it left black streaks behind, it was most likely a paraffin candle.

Eco-friendly candles are becoming more and more popular for several reasons, aside from the ecological points. Natural wax candles burn up to 50 percent longer and hold on to the essential oil scent better, giving a room a cleaner, fresher fragrance. Also, unlike paraffin candles, they emit 95 percent less soot and pollutants into the air.

There are several alternatives, such as the much more expensive beeswax and soy wax—a relatively new candle in the marketplace. Candle maker Michael Richards invented soy wax in 1991, when he sought a cheaper alternative to beeswax, which can cost up to ten times more than paraffin candles. Richards experimented with a variety of natural waxes and soon ended up with a candle wax that was a mixture of soy and other oils. Soon the mixture would end up being solely soy and, in 2001, the patent for soy candle wax was purchased by Cargill, which now manufactures the natural wax for hundreds of retailers and manufacturers who make these environmentally friendly candles.

Another alternative isn't even a wax-based candle at all: rechargeable candles. One popular brand is called Candela. These portable and rechargeable light sources cast a soft glow just like candles, but are totally safe and do not blow out. After an overnight charging, Candela lights glow for up to five hours, the perfect amount of time for a long party or leisurely dinner party. These lights can be used over and over again. While nothing can beat the real deal of candlelight, I find rechargeable lights useful for luminaires and jack-o-lanterns, when keeping a close eye on candlelight just isn't an option.

Check at the end of this book for a list of places to find both soy and rechargeable candles.

SUMMER SIZZLER

This party is full of the many simple techniques and ideas I've adopted for summer entertaining. Often, I've come up with these eco-friendly and resourceful ideas out of sheer frustration. When cooking in a summer-share rental home, for example, proper cooking equipment can be sparse. Who knew hardwood twigs from the forest could be transformed into hardworking corn-on-the-cob holders? And they are so unexpectedly good-looking, too.

But summer entertaining is also gorgeously simple—just stop off at a farmers market and pick up the freshest, most in-season items available and let them shine all on their own. A crisp apple with warm caramel sauce can be more satisfying than the most complicated dish.

You don't need to cook dinner for a crowd to use these tips; they are perfectly good for any summer night you feel like cooking for yourself or your family.

Naturally Flavored Water

We all know that drinking water is good for us, but frankly, bottle after tasteless bottle can be very boring. The solution is to flavor your own water naturally with real fruits, herbs, and vegetables to give it a subtle, refreshing taste.

Cut strips of cucumber, apple, or sprigs of mint and insert into bottles or pitchers of water. Chill for an hour or so in the refrigerator or in the ice chest to give the flavors a chance to develop. Experiment with different additions, like grapefruit, peaches, limes, and lemons, however it's best to stick with one flavor per bottle.

Simply Green "Cooking": Healthy Frozen Treats

Instead of giving your kids a frozen treat full of sugar and artificial colors and flavors, make your own healthy snacks.

Start with an ice-pop mold set (available at any cooking-supply store) and wooden sticks. Fill the molds with vitamin-fortified flavored waters or electrolyte-filled sports drinks. If you want to add natural energy to the pops, add a drop of vitamin B_{12}, too. Insert sticks and freeze overnight.

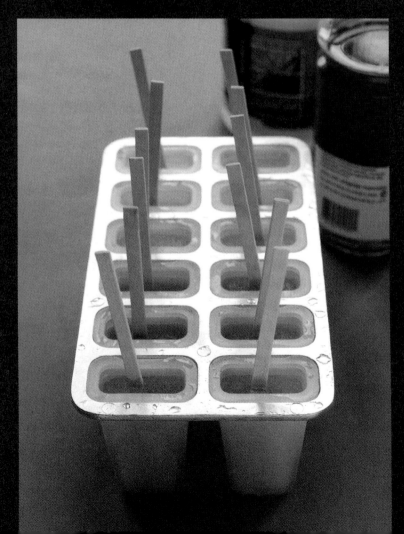

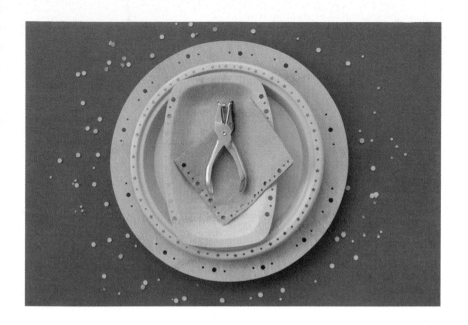

PROJECT: FANCY, ECO-DISPOSABLE PLATES

While using real plates is the best eco-friendly solution, I know in some cases it is not possible. There are some disposable plates that are made from recycled and sustainable materials.

Many of the paper plates found in supermarkets are now made from recycled materials, including the chartreuse-colored one (pictured) from Recycline, which is made from recycled yogurt cups. The large charger plate on the bottom is from Bambu and made from sustainable bamboo; it looks like a wood plate, but it is actually made from a fast-growing grass that is surprisingly durable and good looking.

To dress up these plates, use hole punchers of varying sizes to create a pattern around the edge of the plates. Alternate a large hole with a smaller one, going around the perimeter of the plate. Use other decorative hole punchers as well, to add stars, hearts, and other pretty shapes to your eco-friendly dinnerware. Be creative! You can also use a hole puncher with recycled paper towels to make them into prettier napkins.

PROJECT: PERSONAL HERB POTS

There are decisions in life that are very definitive—the same goes with cilantro. You either love it or hate it.

Instead of garnishing your cooking with herbs that your guests may or may not enjoy, give them options: Provide a custom herb pot at each place setting. Fill a cup with water and a variety of herbs, such as flat-leaf parsley, dill, rosemary, mint, basil, and, of course, cilantro.

Tie a pretty ribbon to a pair of small scissors and let guests customize their soup, salad, entrée, and even dessert.

Tips on Saving Money When Buying Organic

It is true that most organic foods—fresh fruits and vegetables, dairy, eggs, and prepacked foods—do cost more. But the one thing to keep in mind is that organic food means higher-quality food; artisan and handmade touches, smaller batches, obsessive attention to the freshest, most delicious ingredients. I believe organic and gourmet go hand in hand.

But I, too, like saving money and have some tips:

1: Sign up for a free shopper's-club savings card. Many supermarkets have a bonus card program so they can collect valuable data on consumer habits, helping them stock the stores with items their customers actually buy. To reward your loyalty, they often offer discounts throughout the store; these items frequently include the organic items, often at very steep discounts. If you see a good deal, stock up.

2. Store brands can save you money. Decades ago, supermarkets created "no-frills brands" that lacked expensive packaging, and passed the savings on to the consumer. These generic items were easily identifiable by their plain, black-and-white packaging. Today, supermarkets have evolved generic into store brands. These are high-quality, gourmet varieties of popular items like soy milk, chocolates, olive oil, canned beans, frozen fruits and vegetables, and much more, often made from organic ingredients at lower prices. The store-brand organic soy milk I drink is actually cheaper than the lowest-priced regular milk!

3. Search the Internet. Many organic food companies offer printable coupons available on their Web sites.

4. Buy in bulk. Warehouse clubs are beginning to carry a wide variety of eco-friendly household items (recycled paper towels, cleaning supplies) and organic food items; larger quantities up-front, mean bigger savings at the register. Consider buying the essentials you will always need: cold-pressed organic olive oil, recycled paper toilet tissue, a big bag of organic lemons (if you are planning to make freshly squeezed lemonade for a party, etc.).

DRINKING-STRAW ALTERNATIVE

Plastic drinking straws can take hundreds of years to biodegrade. There is a better and tastier alternative.

To make Twizzlers candy into yummy straws, all you have to do is snip the ends, insert, and sip. Serve them in spiked punch in tall glasses. This is also a lovely addition to a children's party; kids can drink their beverages and then eat the straw.

Tip: Twizzlers now come in a wide variety of flavors. Try chocolate Twizzlers with chocolate or regular organic milk, strawberry Twizzlers with—yep, you guessed it—strawberry milk. For grown-ups, use licorice-flavored Twizzler with Sambuca, an anise-flavored liquor.

PROJECT: OYSTER-SHELL TEA LIGHTS

Materials

Oyster shells

Newspaper

Cardboard box

Microwaveable soy wax

Pyrex measuring cup

Pre-tabbed, 2-inch candlewicks (available at any craft store)

Tray

Small pebbles, dried beans, or uncooked rice

After dining on freshly shucked oysters at your favorite restaurant, ask the waiter to pack them up so you can bring them home. They will make great nautical-inspired tea lights.

First, scrub the shells in warm, sudsy water; set aside on a dish towel to dry completely. Crumble some newspaper and place it in a cardboard box; steady the oyster shells on top of the newspaper so they are completely level. This will help to avoid spillage when pouring the hot wax into the shells. Microwave the soy wax in the measuring cup according to package instructions; once melted, dip the pre-tabbed candlewicks in the hot wax and insert in the middle of each shell. Pour the melted wax into each shell and allow to cool.

Before lighting the tea lights, steady them on a tray lined with small pebbles, dried beans, or uncooked rice, as I've done here. This will help catch any melted wax and help make cleanup a breeze.

PROJECT: SCENTED PAPER FLOWERS

Materials

Magazine scent-strip advertisements

Newspaper

Floral wire

Floral tape

Scissors

Can you imagine giving a bouquet of lovely flowers that smell just like the recipient's favorite perfume?

This bouquet of flowers is actually made from the scent strips found in fashion and beauty magazines—and they are a cinch to make.

1. Remove perfume advertisements from the magazine and cut out the perfume strips plus an inch of the non-scented paper.

2. Fold this piece of paper in half lengthwise and then again. Using a pair of scissors, cut a petal out of the paper, using as much of the scented part as possible. Be sure to add a "tab" at the bottom of the petal so you can easily attach the petals to the florist wire.

3. Attach the scented petals to the wire with floral tape, twisting the wire while slightly pulling the tape (which will release the glue on the tape). Finish by adding the four unscented petals cut from the rest of the advertisement.

4. Roll a sheet of newspaper into a cone and fill with shredded newspaper and insert the bouquet of scented flowers. The scent will last for weeks.

PROJECT: MOSQUITO REPELLANT CARRYING TINS

Materials

Stainless-steel bento box

2 pounds of microwaveable soy wax

Pyrex measuring cup

Approximately 50 drops of citronella oil

Pre-tabbed candlewicks

I love finding new uses for everyday objects. This project uses a modern-day bento box in a fresh and useful way.

In Japan, bento is a prepared lunch made at home and taken to work by both adults and children. Today, these lunches are often carried in simple, stainless-steel stackable containers, usually with three to four individual compartments, all held together by a metal brace that also acts as a handy carrier.

There are a myriad of modern uses for these inexpensive steel bento boxes, which can be found at many Asian markets. One idea is to make a set of traveling citronella candles so you can keep mosquitoes away no matter where your outdoor party may be.

Microwave the soy wax in the measuring cup according to package instructions. Once melted, add the citronella oil and stir. Dip a candlewick into the hot wax and center in one of the steel compartments; slowly pour the hot wax and fill to desired height. Allow to cool completely.

You can make candles in all the compartments (as pictured here), or fill two of the compartments and use the third one to carry other outdoor essentials: bug spray and matches.

REFRESHING AND CLEANSING HAND TOWELS

Summertime heat and humidity can leave hands feeling sticky. Treat your guests to a cooling hand towel before dinner.

Squeeze one whole lemon into a bowl of ice water. Soak the hand towels in the water for a few minutes and then gently ring them out. Roll them up on a tray and chill in the freezer or refrigerator. Before serving, place a lemon slice on top of each towel. The towels will clean hands, while the lemon juice will disinfect.

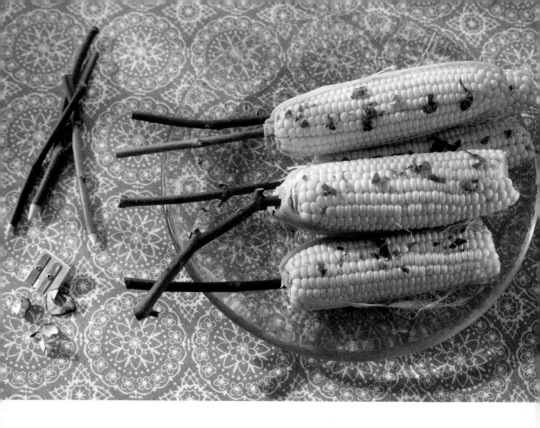

TWIG CORN–ON–THE–COB HOLDERS

There's no need to purchase corn-on-the-cob holders when Mother Nature can come to the rescue.

Clip fresh twigs from trees and sharpen the ends in a pencil sharpener. Insert the twigs into the ends of the corn and grill them up.

PROJECT: SHOPPING-BAG BASKETS

A simple shopping bag can be recycled into a charming paper basket with just a few snips of the scissors.

Choose small, colorful paper bags and snip the left and right top corners out of the bag; leave a strip about 1 inch wide, and the middle intact. Use double-stick tape or glue to attach the two tabs together to make a handle.

Place small containers inside the bag (used plastic deli containers, for example), fill with water, and then arrange some fresh flowers. Choose flowers and greenery that complement the colors of the bag.

Party 6

WINTER
WARM-UP PARTY

I have started an annual tradition where I invite my close friends over for a long, three-day weekend at the end of fall to welcome winter. I whip up a comforting roasted butternut squash soup, make sweet and savory salads, and even spice up the freshly brewed organic coffee. In preparation for their arrival, the beds are dressed with warm flannel sheets and the duvets are stuffed with Ingeo fiber comforters (an alternative to down feathers). I even keep a basket of warm socks near the bed in case it gets too cold. From the basement, I bring up a seasonal set of dining room chairs—dark walnut chairs covered in the warmest wool and cashmere-blend fabrics.

Even when it's too cold to dine outside, you can still have a great time indoors with the ideas in this chapter. Warm up to this new tradition and invite your friends over to say hello to Jack Frost.

Garden-Urn Dining Table

This hardworking, metal planter is used to showcase an impressive group-ing of greenery and flowers in the summer. In the winter, give it a new use as a handsome, stable base for a dining room table.

Use a metal urn that is between 32 to 36 inches in height. Place a solid marble slab on top (this circular one was purchased from a vintage fur-niture store), and center it. You can add a caulk lining on top of the urn to secure the marble, but here the sheer weight of the marble keeps the entire piece sturdy and steady.

Tip: Don't search for metal urns at home-improvement stores or garden centers. The faux finish ones, while inexpensive, won't hold up to the weight of the marble and the real iron ones will be very expensive. Instead, search junk stores and flea markets for them. Because of the urns' heavy weight, many vendors will be more willing to haggle on price since it'll be a bigger burden to them to repack and rehaul the heavy piece.

PROJECT: SWEATER CHAIRS

Materials

Old sweaters

Chairs with removable seat cushions

Screwdriver

Scissors

Staple gun

A good sign of a successful dinner party is when you and your guests linger for hours around a dinner table sharing stories, drinking wine, and just having a wonderful time. One way to encourage conversation late into the night, is to reupholster your chairs with old sweaters to make them more comfortable, if not totally indulgent.

This is a great way to recycle a cherished cashmere or wool sweater that has seen better days. Be sure to choose a sweater that is large enough to cover the seat cushion of the chair.

Using a screwdriver, start by unscrewing the seat cushion from the chair; there are usually four screws underneath holding it in place. Be sure to save the screws so you can reattach the seat cushion later.

Cut the sweater open with a pair of scissors so it becomes one large, flat piece of fabric. Place the seat cushion on top and wrap the sweater around it. Secure the sweater to the chair by stapling it to the bottom of the seat; trim the excess fabric. Screw the cushion back into the chair.

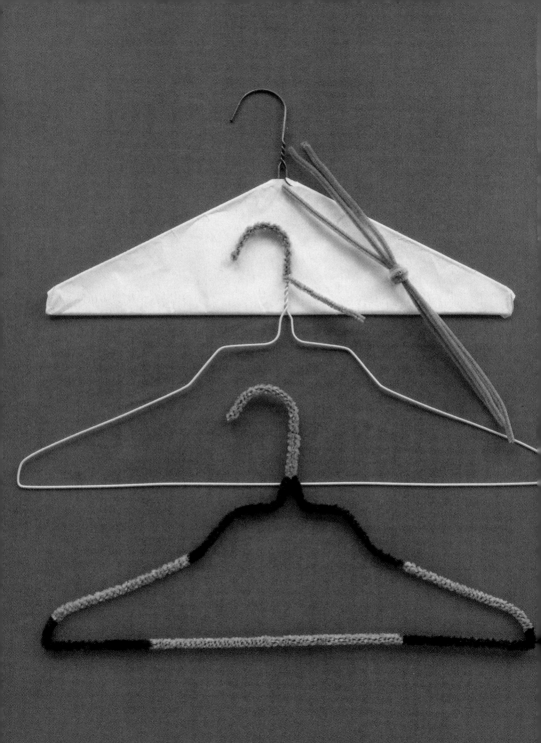

PROJECT: FUZZY HANGERS

Recycle flimsy wire hangers into warm and fuzzy creations in just one simple step. All you need is an array of pipe cleaners in a variety of pretty colors. Just twist the pipe cleaners around the frame of the hanger; use contrasting colors for a striped effect. The end result is a hanger that is stronger, softer, and slip-proof.

Tip: Pipe cleaners now come in a wide variety of colors, finishes, and sizes. Visit your local craft store, look at all the choices, and stick to one "theme" for all your hangers so they match. Try metallic pipe cleaners for a modern look, or use the same color for a monochromatic collection.

PROJECT: SCARF QUILT

Old scarves

Large needle

Yarn

The Amish of Pennsylvania are world renowned for their intricate and beautiful handmade quilts. These masterpieces often involve several people dedicating hundreds of hours of meticulous sewing just to make one quilt.

Inspired by this centuries-old tradition, I came up with a simple, modern approach to quilting that recycles old woolen winter scarves into a beautiful striped blanket. While it pales in comparison to the Amish masterpieces, the finished scarf-blanket can still keep you warm on a cold night.

Thread a large needle with a colorful piece of yarn; if the scarves have a mostly neutral color palette, a brightly colored yarn will add an unexpected dash of energy to the finished blanket. Sew two of the scarves together by running a simple stitch back and forth between them.

Depending on the width of the scarves, you will need approximately five to six scarves to make a large enough blanket. Also, if you don't have the time to stitch the scarves together, ask a local tailor who can usually sew them up in a jiffy for very little money. There is incredible versatility with a scarf-blanket: store one in the car to keep passengers warm, offer one as a handmade gift, or even pull one out in the summertime to serve as a picnic blanket.

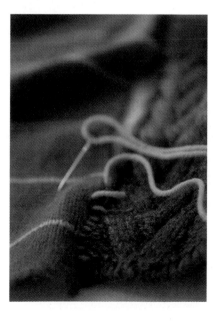

PROJECT: PEBBLE POTPOURRI

Some of the best things are the simplest. It may be cold and snowy outside, but it can smell fresh and summery indoors.

Toss a handful of pebbles with a fragrant essential oil of your choice; try lavender, peppermint, or rose. Add some crystal chandelier pieces for a glitzy touch. Display in a serving dish in the middle of the table, and let the natural scent perfume the room.

PROECT: REGLAZED SILHOUETTE PLATES

Thrift shop or unwanted ceramic plates

8½-by-11-inch inkjet sticker project paper

Scissors

Foam brushes

Rubbing alcohol

Porcelain paint

This project is an excellent example of resourcefulness: turning something ordinary into a thing of beauty.

A visit to any Goodwill store will lead you to a treasure trove of plates in unusual patterns, available for pennies. Also, your own home may have stacks of unwanted ceramic tableware full of outdated floral and kitschy patterns—perhaps passed down from another generation—that clash with today's simpler, cleaner table settings.

Like a chipped piece of furniture in need of a good coat of paint, consider reglazing these plates into gorgeous new pieces.

Print an image off the computer of a silhouette you find pleasing on sticker project paper; choose a shape that is easily identifiable. I chose this simple image of a cow and enlarged it to fit the size of the plate.

With a pair of scissors, cut out the image, peel off the protective backing, and adhere it to the center of the plate. With a foam brush, clean the exposed surface with rubbing alcohol. Once dry, brush a coat of porcelain paint on the plate. You may need several coats of paint, depending how dark you want the glaze to be. Allow to dry overnight.

Peel off the image from the plate and place it in the oven. Heat it to 350 degrees and bake the plate for 25 minutes. Turn off the oven and allow the plate to cool completely inside the oven. Your handmade plates are hand-washable only.

PROJECT: PERSONALIZED FLAVORED COFFEES

Since most flavored coffees are full of artificial flavors and aren't made from organic beans, the solution is to make your own brew at home. By blending your own naturally flavored coffees, you can customize the taste perfectly to your liking.

Add fresh hazelnuts, chili peppers, cinnamon sticks, cayenne pepper, or cocoa nibs to whole coffee beans right before grinding. A little goes a long way, so be conservative when adding.

Good for the Planet—
to the Last Drop

For decades, coffee was grown under the canopy of the rich rain forest, helping to keep complex biodiversity intact while still being a working farm. A few decades ago, scientists developed a new type of coffee bush that delivered much higher yields, but demanded full-sun growing conditions to thrive. Because these new hybrid bushes would give the farmer more income, rain forests were cut and fertilized for these new coffee farms. The result of such clear-cutting are devastating: mudslides, loss of natural habitat, and unknown global effects from the loss of valuable rain forest land.

Today, ecologically minded consumers are choosing shade-grown, organic coffee instead of conventional java. The older varieties of the coffee bush—much like an heirloom tomato today—are being brought back and grown under the protective canopy of the rain forest. The results of supporting these farmers are twofold: You're supporting farmers who choose sustainable techniques, and you're helping to protect the delicate biodiversity of the rainforest. One hundred fifty migratory birds, for example, call these coffee farms home, an ecological oasis to them, while a regular, full-sun farm has almost no birds. A shade-grown coffee farm that thrives also conserves the land for future generations.

This type of progressive farming usually means fair treatment to workers, too. "Fair trade coffee" is a label often seen on organic and shade-grown coffee bags. Fair trade means just like it says: Coffee growers are paid a premium for their coffee beans.

While the cost of shade-grown, organic coffee may cost a few dollars more, for true java lovers, the price is worth it. Not only is it a green choice, but many connoisseurs agree that shade-grown coffee is superior in taste: less bitter with a more concentrated flavor. It's easy to find these coffee beans at your local coffeehouse or supermarket: Just read the label. If it's certified organic, there is a very good chance it is also shade-grown coffee.

PROJECT: SALAD-BAR RADISH ROSES

One dozen organic roses

Oasis (a florist foam that absorbs water)

Small watertight bowls

Pruning shears

Outdoor greenery

One bunch of radishes

Toothpicks

Think roses are too expensive for a casual centerpiece on the table? Here's an economical and ecological idea to stretch a dozen roses even further.

Make sure to use organic roses (available at most organic-food supermarkets and online); if you can't find organic, conventional is fine, but keep in mind they have been sprayed with herbicides and insecticides.

Soak a block of Oasis foam in water for several minutes. After soaking, cut the Oasis foam to size so it fits snugly in the watertight bowl. Using pruning shears, snip the roses so you have a 2-inch stem on each flower. Insert several roses (I used four in each bowl to create three small arrangements), and fill in any empty spaces with outdoor greenery, such as boxwood leaves or holly. Remove the greens from the radishes and poke a toothpick through the top of each radish, leaving the decorative "root" exposed. Fill in the spaces in the arrangement with the radishes; the toothpicks will keep them in place.

After the party, toss some fresh rose petals into a jar of sugar; it will lightly scent the sugar with the floral sweetness of the roses.

Why Organic Roses?

It often comes as a surprise to people to learn something so beautiful can also be so toxic.

Almost all the roses you see artfully styled in gorgeous arrangements have been heavily sprayed with toxic pesticides and fertilizers. This poisonous cocktail not only stays on the flowers, but also leaks into waterways at the farm, affecting the natural biodiversity of the surrounding habitats. Workers on these farms have also been harmed by the high levels

of chemicals, and they often get sick from working with flowers. Even the neighborhood florist is prone to sickness; there has been alarming occurrences among florists who handle nonorganic flowers developing dermatitis on their hands. Why do these farmers grow flowers in such toxic conditions? The answer is simple: to achieve perfect flowers, for perfect arrangements, that arrive perfectly to you. Flowers are a commodity, and flower farmers want to make sure their investments are fully protected. But is the trade-off worth it to achieve the perfect rose?

To understand, start by thinking about the last time you smelled a rose growing in a garden, its delicately beautiful fragrance emanating from the petals. Then when you visit the supermarket, smell a bouquet of roses; they will not smell. It's no mistake. Today, many commercial roses are bred (read: genetically modified) for their stem strength and longevity; the scent of the rose is sacrificed to make the flowers more durable. They are gorgeous to look at, but lack scent altogether. It has gotten so bad that many florists are now spraying roses with artificial fragrance.

The solution to this madness is organic roses. Surprisingly, it's not environmentalists who have started the trend, but it's pastry chefs and gourmet chefs. In recent years, cooking with fresh roses has become a growing trend. But to safely cook with roses—whether it's a rose-scented sorbet or crystallized rose petals on cupcakes—they must be organic. As more food lovers are willing to pay a premium for organic roses to be included in their culinary masterpieces, more farmers are willing to grow them. It's simple: If farmers can make more money from fragrant, organic roses, they'll plant them. The growth of organic roses is also starting to trickle into the consumer marketplace. You can find bouquets of organic roses online at organicbouquet.com or at better-known health-food stores like Whole Foods and Wild Oats.

117

PROJECT: ROCK PLACE CARDS

Why spend money at the card store on throw-away place cards when you can make your own in seconds?

Borrow beautiful polished stones from your yard or the park, and write your guests' names directly on them. For a more artistic result, use an alphabet stamp set and an ink pad. Place a colorful leaf underneath to continue the outdoors theme. When the party is over, wipe off the names and return the stones back to where you found them.

Tip: If you have out-of-town guests, consider having them sign their rock place card, including the date and a sweet message. Save these rocks in a large apothecary jar, and collect signed rocks from guests all year round.

119

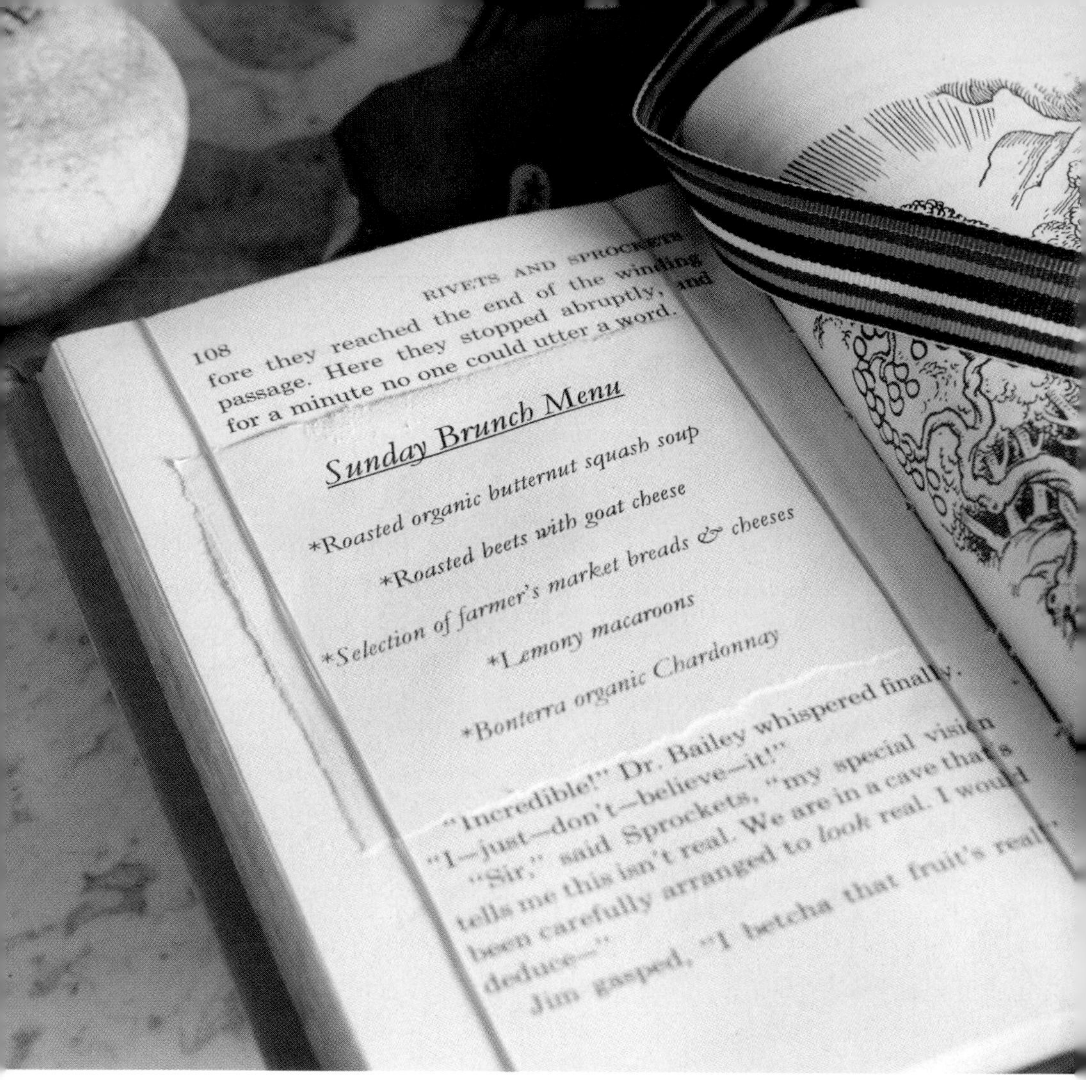

108 fore they reached the end of the winding passage. Here they stopped abruptly, and for a minute no one could utter a word.

Sunday Brunch Menu

*Roasted organic butternut squash soup

*Roasted beets with goat cheese

*Selection of farmer's market breads & cheeses

*Lemony macaroons

*Bonterra organic Chardonnay

"Incredible!" Dr. Bailey whispered finally. "I—just—don't—believe—it!"

"Sir," said Sprockets, "my special vision tells me this isn't real. We are in a cave that's been carefully arranged to look real. I would deduce—"

Jim gasped, "I betcha that fruit's real!

PROJECT: BOOK MENUS

Even for a casual get-together, it's nice to let guests know what they will be having for dinner. Here I used a vintage hardcover book as a menu. Don't worry: No book is harmed in the process.

Print out the menu from your computer on recycled paper. Cut the menu to size, and insert it inside the book. Use two large, colorful rubber bands to hold the menu in place. The rubber bands will also direct the guests to the exact page containing the evening's meal.

Tip: Charming illustrated vintage books don't have to come from a pricey antiquarian bookstore. Books from the 60s and 70s can often be found in the bargain bins at thrift stores. Local libraries also have book sales as fund-raisers, so be on the lookout for the next sale and stock up on quirky and interesting books.

Simply Green Cooking: Roasted Butternut Squash Soup

This is my no-fail, butternut squash soup recipe. It's quick and easy, and the perfect warm dish to serve on a chilly day. This recipe is so simple, you'll wonder why you ever bought canned soup.

INGREDIENTS

- Two large organic butternut squash, halved and seeded
- 8 cloves of garlic, peeled
- 4 tablespoons of extra-virgin olive oil
- 32-ounce container of organic vegetable broth
- Salt and pepper
- ¼ cup maple syrup
- Fresh dill (optional)

1. Preheat the oven to 400 degrees. Line a baking sheet with unbleached parchment paper.

2. Cut squash in half, lengthwise. Scoop out the seeds and discard. Place two cloves of garlic in the cavity of each squash. Place the squash, flesh side down, on the baking sheet. Roast until tender, about 30 minutes, depending on the size of the squash.

3. Remove squash from the oven and allow them to cool for about 15 minutes. Heat up the olive oil in a large stockpot over medium-high heat. Using a large spoon, scoop out the flesh of each squash directly into the stockpot; add the cooked garlic. Add half of the vegetable broth and stir; continue adding broth until you reach the desired consistency. Add generous pinches of salt and pepper.

4. Using a handheld blender, puree the soup until smooth, adding more broth if needed. Add the maple syrup. Serve immediately with fresh sprigs of dill on top, if desired.

PROJECT: INCENSE-TO-GO

Small matchbox

Decorative paper (e.g., pretty wrapping-paper remnants)

Decoupage glue

⅛ inch hole puncher

Incense sticks

Sharp scissors

The fragrant smell of incense can go anywhere with you in this handy, easy-to-make traveling incense kit.

Start with a small matchbox and glue decorative paper on the top, bottom, and sides, being careful to leave the "strike" part of the box free of paper. Allow to dry. Punch a hole in the middle of the box with the hole puncher.

Cut down the incense sticks to the same size of the matches; remove enough matches to accommodate the sticks inside the box. To use, pull the box drawer out and insert an incense stick into the hole, making sure it's secured. Strike a match and light the incense, and blow out the flame; it will slowly burn and release fragrance into the air.

Be sure to make extra incense kits since your friends are going to want one.

Simply Green and Sweetly Scented

The guests are just an hour or so away from arriving, the food is cooked, and the wine is chilled. Everything is perfect except for one thing: Your home has a lingering smell. Maybe it's from that richly spiced trout you cooked the night before, or perhaps from a decomposing treat left by your cat somewhere in the house.

To get your house smelling nice and sweet, try these simple tips. There's no need to mask the smell with nauseating and toxic air fresheners.

- Go straight to the source. Food items often get trapped underneath or behind refrigerators, stoves, and other appliances. Once, in my kitchen, there was an awful smell so I cleaned it top to bottom but to no avail; it wasn't until I moved the fridge that I found a bag of lima beans molding away. Move your appliances and sleuth around; give the area a good cleaning and vacuum up any crumbs or runaway food bits.

- Rip open scent strips from magazines, and place them on a warm radiator. The warmth will activate the scent and help perfume the air.

- Slice some lemons in half and squeeze the juice into a heavy-duty pot. Fill the pot with water and spices—cinnamon sticks, cloves, star anise—and let it slowly simmer on the stove.

- Mist the air with a natural scent. Grab the bottle of linen mister from your bedroom, and spray all over the house. Many linen misters come in gentle scents like lavender and rose and are free of artificial additives.

- Deodorize the refrigerator by placing a bowl of charcoal inside. Fill a decorative bowl with charcoal straight from the grill. Since charcoal is very porous, it has natural properties that allow it to absorb moisture and other chemical substances. Also, put charcoal pieces inside closets to absorb excess moisture.

- Sprinkle baking soda all over a carpet and let it sit for an hour or so. The soda will absorb odors and any excess crumbs or stains in the carpet. Vacuum it all up before the party begins.

SIMPLY GREEN SHOPPING:
WHERE TO FIND EVERYTHING YOU NEED

Just a few years ago, if I wanted to buy laundry detergent that was environmentally friendly, I had to order it from a catalog and wait a few weeks. The times have changed! Today, I can stop by almost any major retailer and many local stores and not only find green cleaning supplies, but a *choice* of products, all at competitive prices. You can also find a huge selection of eco-friendly products, including organic gourmet foods, bedding, beauty products, candles, lightbulbs . . . just about everything!

When looking for eco-friendly products, be a label reader. Look for words like "biodegradable," "organic," and "recycled." These buzzwords are a good place to start. Read brochures in the stores that outline the company's social responsibility guidelines; they often list the green products it sells. Ask store employees for help.

Don't always think new: Goodwill, Salvation Army, and flea markets are great places to find vintage dishes, tableware, and place settings. I once found charming vintage holiday cards, still in their packaging, on sale at a thrift shop for just ten cents that I sent out to the delight of my friends. As the saying goes, one man's trash is another man's treasure. Reusing something old is probably the most environmentally friendly choice you can make, and you'll be saving a bundle in the process.

For the more hard-to-find green items that I talk about in this book, here's a directory of manufacturers and retailers that I patronize.

Baby Clothes

Organic baby are a growing trend in the eco-fashion industry.
I think it's perhaps because parents are obsessed with having
only the cleanest, purest things for their little ones to wear.
Colorful, fun, and easy-to-source organic items are coming
up everywhere. Here are a few of my favorite places.

Ecobaby, www.ecobaby.com

Gaiam, www.gaiam.com

Giggle, www.egiggle.com

Under the Nile, www.underthenile.com

Bamboo Plates

Sustainable and fast-growing bamboo seems to be popping
up everywhere! From beautiful flooring to furniture and even
to bamboo shoots in Asian dishes. Bamboo also makes for an
ecological and convenient material when you need disposable
plates.

Bambu, www.bambuhome.com, and Whole Foods and
Dean & Deluca stores nationwide

Burlap

Burlap to a gardener is what muslin is to a fashion designer:
a must-have inexpensive fabric with myriad uses. For my baby
shower chapter, I used burlap to wrap the baby trees, but you
can also use it as a table runner, for outdoor curtains, or even
to reupholster a chair for a rustic look. Really, the ideas are
endless.

Home Depot, www.homedepot.com

Cleaning Supplies

Thankfully, eco-friendly cleaning supplies no longer means mean spritzing a soiled countertop with glorified floral water. Today, green cleaning supplies smell great, clean great, and are easy to find. My favorite brand is Method.

Method, www.methodhome.com and at Target stores nationwide

Cocoa Bean Hull Mulch

I grew up near Hershey, Pennsylvania, the "chocolate capital of the world" and remember the air smelling like chocolate on days with the right breeze. Now you can bring the scent of chocolate to your own garden with this very useful, sweet-smelling mulch.

National Cocoa Shell, www.nationalcocoashell.com

Craft Supplies

All the craft supplies in this book were purchased from two national craft supply retailers: A. C. Moore and Michaels. They seem to have locations everywhere, but if no branches exist in your area, check out your local craft store for the same supplies. I tried my very best to use only things that are truly easy to source.

A. C. Moore, www.acmoore.com

Michaels, www.michaels.com

I store all my craft supplies in a Sears Craftsman canvas tool bag; www.sears.com

Essential Oils

I am absolutely obsessed with essential oils and think their pure, heavenly scent makes even ho-hum chores (e.g., dishwashing) just a tiny bit more relaxing. Store them in a metal tin and have fun using them.

Aveda Singular Notes, www.aveda.com

Bath & Body Works essential oils, www.bathandbodyworks.com

Glow-in-the-Dark Paint

This type of specialty paint is easiest to find right before Halloween, when most crafters use it to give their jack-o'-lanterns an eerie glow. It's found in most craft supply stores, but if you need it sometime other than Halloween, try the web address below.

Glow, Inc., www.glowinc.com

Hand Towels

Sure, the lure of getting a pack of hand towels for next to nothing at a discount retailer is tempting, but please take the extra *Simply Green* step and pick some good-quality ones from the following vendors. Trust me, there is a difference that's worth the wait and extra money.

Anna Sova, www.annasova.com

Coyuchi, www.coyuchi.com

Gaiam, www.gaiam.com

Hemp Cord and String

Hemp string is not only an eco-friendly choice, but it's a strong material, too. Hemp is 1 ½ times stronger than cotton, which basically means that whatever you make with it will last longer.

Available in the jewelry-making section of any craft store.

Hemp Fabric

Hey, the same 1 ½ times-stronger rule applies to fabric, too!

Hemp Traders, www.hemptraders.com

Indika, www.indikahome.com

Leather Rotary Punch

Okay, you know how I said everything I used is a cinch to find? I meant everything except this *one* item. A leather rotary punch is a must-have if you plan on doing anything with leather. It's not terribly expensive, and it will make your leather crafting so much easier.

eLeatherSupply, www.eleathersupply.com

Polished Pebbles

You might be wondering, "Why buy rocks when they are everywhere in the front yard?" Because Smith & Hawken sells rocks that are so pretty, you'll want to display them inside the house and not outside. Pick up a bag at a store nearest you.

Smith & Hawken; visit www.smithandhawken.com for store locations.

Rechargeable "Candles"

My client, the Kimpton Hotel Group, has these in some of its properties, and I adore them. They glow just like candles, but there's no fire to deal with. Charge them up and put them inside luminaires, make a pathway with them, or just set them on a table.

Vessel, Inc. (Candela), www.vesselinc.com

Recycled Plastic Plates

Who knew plastic disposable plates could be eco-friendly. The folks at Recycline sure came up with a win-win product for both the time-pressed consumer *and* the planet.

Recycline, www.recycline.com

Roses

I talk about this company so much on my radio show that I've often been asked if I have a personal business stake it! I think they sell only fabulous, richly scented roses free of any chemical pesticides—like fresh-picked from the garden. And, *no*, I do not have a stake!

Organic Bouquet, www.organicbouquet.com, and in select Whole Foods stores

Shade-Grown Coffee

I can't taste the difference between shade-grown and conventional coffee, but I do think grinding eco-friendly beans is a nice way to start the day. It's sorta Zenful to be half awake each morning thinking, "Well, at least I didn't destroy the rainforest for this cup of joe."

Green Mountain Coffee, www.greenmountaincoffee.com

Organic Coffee Company, www.organiccoffeecompany.com
Starbucks organic, shade-grown, and fair-trade coffees,
www.starbucksstore.com

Solar Lighting

You can find solar lighting at virtually any home-improvement store these days. So be a high-maintenance design freak and seek out the coolest, most attractive solar lights you can find.
Gardener's Supply Company, www.gardeners.com
Real Goods, www.realgoods.com;
Target, www.target.com

Soy Candles

I predict that one day, soy candles will be so common in home-decorating stores that placement in a resource section like this will be obsolete. Soy candles have so many benefits that it's only a matter of time before people ditch those awful petroleum-based ones for good!
Ergo Candles, www.ergocandle.com
Gaiam, www.gaiam.com
Natural Wax Candle Company, www.itsasoy.com

Soy Wax

And until that day—whenever you need to make your own soy candles—give this company a try for the raw wax.
Yaley Enterprises, Inc., www.yaley.com

Tea

I'm not a huge tea drinker, but everyone who visits me for the weekend seems to drink only tea, so I always keep plenty on hand. Find good organic teas in exotic varieties, and store them in a cool, dark place.

Republic of Tea, www.republicoftea.com

Wine

These days, many wine shops have a section labeled "organic," just as they have sections for type and region. Here are some easy-to-find wines that I like:

Bonterra Vineyards, www.bonterra.com

Frey Vineyards, www.freywine.com

Frog's Leap, www.frogsleap.com

Index

"Danny Seo's passion, integrity, and commitment to creating a better world are inspiring, and his fresh ideas are actually making a difference."

—David Lauren, Vice President, Polo Ralph Lauren

"Danny's incredibly creative ideas make green living sexy, fabulous, and fun!"

—Kerry Washington

"Danny marries style with concern for the environment, fun with resourcefulness . . . and pulls it all off with ease. Throw your next celebration with this book; you can't go wrong."

—Amy Smart

Danny Seo is America's environmental lifestyle expert on stylish, eco-friendly living. He is the author of four books, including *Conscious Style Home: Eco-Friendly Living for the 21st Century*. Danny is the host, creator, and executive producer of the TV series *Simply Green with Danny Seo*, on LIME: *Healthy Living with a Twist*, and host of the companion program of the same name on SIRIUS Satellite Radio. He is a contributing editor to *Country Home* magazine, and his work on eco-friendly style has appeared in *USA*

Today, People, Elle, Food & Wine, Parade, and on *The Oprah Winfrey Show, The View,* and *Today.* Danny is the spokesperson for "Call2Recycle," a nationwide, nonprofit cell phone and rechargeable battery recycling campaign. He is also the official eco-stylist for Kimpton Hotels, a collection of upscale, boutique properties nationwide. Danny proudly supports the Humane Society of the United States. Learn more at www.dannyseo.com.

Jennifer Levy is a New York–based photographer specializing in lifestyle, design, and food. Her work appears in numerous magazines, including *Metropolitan Home, Martha Stewart Living,* and *Better Homes and Gardens.* She has photographed more than 14 books and was both photographer and author of *Kids' Rooms: Ideas and Projects for Children's Spaces* (Chronicle, 2001). In addition to photography assignments, her current project is the design and renovation of a Brooklyn town house, which—should she survive—will house herself, her partner (filmmaker Art Jones), and her son, Edison.

Watch
simply green with
Danny on the LIME
network:
healthy living with
a twist and on
LIME.com.